CONSEQUENCES

First published in 1991 by Absolute Classics, an imprint of
Absolute Press, 14 Widcombe Crescent, Bath, England

Cover and text design: Ian Middleton

Photoset and printed by The Longdunn Press Ltd, Bristol
Bound by W.H. Ware & Son, Clevedon

ISBN 0 948230 46 0

All rights in this play are strictly reserved and application for
performances should be made in advance before the beginning of
rehearsals to The Gate theatre, 11 Pembridge Road, Notting Hill,
London W11.

CONSEQUENCES

Act One
Scene One: Tariq Ali
Scene Two: Ranjit Bolt
Scene Three: Adrian Mitchell
Scene Four: Michael Meyer
Scene Five: Nick Dear

Act Two
Scene One: Arnold Wesker
Scene Two: Frank McGuinness
Scene Three: Nicholas Wright
Scene Four: Richard Curtis
Scene Five: Tariq Ali

a b s o l u t e   c l a s s i c s

INTRODUCTION

CONSEQUENCES - THE PLOT

'Dear Playwright,
As you know, The Gate in Notting Hill has pursued a policy of producing
premières of European plays in translation for over a decade now, as well
as staging a wide range of innovative international work, creating a
World Theatre repertoire for British Theatre. Yet, despite this
contribution of fine productions, involving leading theatre practitioners
and attracting widespread critical acclaim, The Gate still receives no
public funding.

In order to develop our literary work – to establish a Literary Department
and to help found an International Script Union – we have initiated an
ambitious and exciting way to raise the necessary money. We are asking
major writers to contribute to a play: CONSEQUENCES. We hope that
you will be interested in being involved. Each writer has a fortnight to
compose their short scene independently of the other writers but picking up
the play where the previous writer left off. The first writer will be drawn
out of a hat; the second will see the first writer's draft; the third the first
and second's draft, and so on. Each person is invited to write in the style
of a foreign writer, playfully developing the story, themes, and/or
characters established by the previous writers, in terms of consequences.
There is no limit to the number of characters each writer wishes to
introduce to, or kill off from, the pre-existing cast-list. The ticket sales
from a gala performance of the finished play will raise money for The
Gate's literary work.

We appreciate how busy you must be, but we do hope that you will be
willing to take part. Our plans for a Literary Department depend on
raising the financial resources. Once established, we would be able to
extend our commissioning of translations and adaptations of foreign work.
And CONSEQUENCES itself will inspire other writers to tackle
neglected foreign plays' . . .

And so we wrote to a variety of playwrights, adaptors, versionists and
translators – some of whom were all four, all of whom were proven
talents, and none of whose work had ever played at The Gate. Our
audacity was slow to pay off. Having sent out the initial letters at the
end of July 1990, a steady stream of responses arrived on the doormat:
'The thought of producing five pages within two weeks petrifies me';
'I'd be hopeless at it'; 'I . . . must . . . be . . . excused . . . I . . . write

. . . at . . . a . . . snail's . . . pace'. Encouraging though they were (only one writer returned a dismissive missive on a postcard bearing a bare woman's behind) most writers felt that they couldn't take the pressure. But then some – intrigued by the game on the one hand, appreciative of the necessity of adventurism in the face of poverty on the other – telephoned, or wrote, to say: 'By all means cast me into your *Consequences* hat'; 'Ready to rock'; or, with eager hope, 'at the moment I'm snowed up here in the hills. But snow melts, doesn't it?'

This is the spirit of The Gate. It rubbed off on the typewriters of nine highly accomplished writers who, suspending posh commissions, composed their pithy scenes.

The play is a unique creation. It can also be seen as an historical document. Towards the end of 1990, The Young Vic in The Cut spearheaded a campaign to Save our Theatres (and implicitly Britain's dramatic culture). The Gate would never be affected by The Cuts, since we had nothing to lose. Constant acknowledgement from peer group and press reports (as diverse as 'City Limits', 'The Tablet', 'The Daily Telegraph' and BBC Radio's 'Woman's Hour') doesn't seem to attract the attention of funding bodies. Sponsors have seen the attraction: our Women in World Theatre Season, six plays from four continents in the first five months of 1991, would not have been remotely possible without the support of NatWest, 'Time Out', the Goethe Institute, and Wolff Olins. And when it comes to running the tiny room above the Prince Albert in Notting Hill, Friends of the Gate magnificently make the auditorium a more comfortable space by buying seats and contributing to our Air Conditioning Fund (we're the hottest theatre in town in both senses).

For this, our heartfelt thanks. Everything else – and there's an enormous number of elses – relies on goodwill. One linguist (who reads, translates and advises for our Lope de Vega project for nothing) started to spruce up our front of house, sanding our tiny foyer's floorboards with a sander whose fuse blew, stoically finishing the job on his hands and knees with a scrap of sandpaper. When Peter Brook paid a visit, the Artistic Director nearly missed him because he was scrubbing the bowl of our solitary loo with a kindly donated toothbrush. Unpaid performers heroically squeeze into a dressing-room the size (and still bearing the porcelain) of a gentlemen's urinal. The executive producer/press officer/marketing director/accountant/front-of-house manger/, needless to say the one and the same Caroline Maude, frets away at the end of a hectic day tearing tickets

and squeezing an eager 65-strong audience into a space designed for
56. And our angelic Production Manager, Paul Russell, arrived with a
touring company in September 1990 and hasn't left the theatre since,
rewiring, painting, building through the night to create a modest
palace from a modish pit.

In the short-term, plays will be put on as long as sponsors like us, and
creative and production teams are prepared to accept the conditions.
The theatre and its environs will function as long as a skeleton staff
stay on their toes. We call our own distinctive tune, but no-one pays
this piper. Of course, we're the victims of our own success. The re-
founding of the theatre by Lou Stein in 1979 (Peter Godfrey's Covent
Garden loft between the Wars established The Gate as a pioneer of
foreign plays) and the genius of Giles Croft's European Classics'
policy up until 1989, left Stephen Daldry, the present Artistic
Director, with a strong base from which to launch The Gate into a
decade of expansion, and development, producing fourteen out of
fifteen plays in 1991, from a resource of incredibly neglected world
drama. And that's the *raison d'être*. And that's the point of
CONSEQUENCES.

Like the proverbial lager, The Gate's artistic policy reaches the parts
that other national theatres cannot reach. To put on a play, first it
needs to be found. Naturally, people come to The Gate with exciting
ideas. Obviously, we discover many of our plays for ourselves. In both
cases the process at least involves reading, researching, developing,
translating, commissioning, liaising, contracting, printing, co-
ordinating, discussing, nurturing, editing, being and doing (in no
particular order of merit). In short, a theatre renowned for its foreign
policy needs a foreign office. Hence the Literary Department. Other
theatres have them – other theatres have funding. We have one in a
very embryonic state. We have no money to fund it. The Gate's
policy has been maintained by sustaining a Literary in-tray and out-
tray on the keenness of enthusiasts and a burgeoning writing and
translating community. The Gate needs to establish a Literary
Department both for itself and for the resource it will (and already
informally does) provide for companies up and down the country.
And thanks to the outrageous generosity, refined wit and selfless
creativity of nine writers, an inexhaustible publisher, a theatre
audience and a book-buying public, this is now possible.
CONSEQUENCES is a consequence of an indisputable need for
something most people had always assumed that a theatre of The
Gate's stature must have.

CONSEQUENCES - THE PLAY

When the first scene was written, Margaret Thatcher had just been sent off to the knackers yard (and at The Gate we celebrated with stage-prop champagne drunk from half-pint glasses borrowed from the pub below). But it wasn't her departure which dominated the thoughts of writers during the dawn of 1991 - it was the Gulf Crisis. The form of the play itself, and its very motivation, often become the subject. And as the play progresses, each writer's particular obsession and idiosyncrasy begin to take shape in a curiously cohesive way. No play has ever before, or will ever again, combine such original voices who here cleverly write with an eye on those foreign writers from whom they inherit a tradition and culture of writing for the stage.

So, the scenes are as follows:

Act One

Scene 1 TARIQ ALI - shortly after the première of *Moscow Gold* (which he co-wrote with Howard Brenton) at the RSC's Barbican Theatre - writes in the style of the inimitable Tariq Ali.

Scene 2 RANJIT BOLT's polished translations of Corneille, which have enjoyed such success at the Old Vic and elsewhere, inspire his scene in that 17th century French writer's style of rhyme and reason.

Scene 3 ADRIAN MITCHELL explains his own scene: 'I did start off with Lope de Vega in mind, then Cervantes, but in the end found the only way to write it was in my own style. So, it's in the style of the foreign writer Adrian Mitchell, collaborating with his old mucker Samuel Taylor Coleridge' (a version of *Blood & Oil* first appeared in 'Tribune'; a version of *Ten Holes for a Soldier* was first published in 'The Guardian').

Scene 4 MICHAEL MEYER, legendary translator and biographer of Ibsen and Strindberg, offers a potted parody of Strindberg's *The Father*.

Scene 5 NICK DEAR's *Art Of Success* goes beyond his own original plays to versions of Tirso de Molina (*The Last Days of Don Juan*) and Ostrovsky (with whom he had *A Family Affair* with Cheek by Jowl) - this scene is very much after Ostrovsky.

Act Two

Scene 1 ARNOLD WESKER's theatre *Roots* need no explanation: here he has composed a sophisticated scene which could be attributed to Pirandello.

Scene 2 FRANK McGUINNESS can check off the Cusack *Three Sisters* from his vast output of original plays and adaptations. Here Chekhov unusually meets Raoul Wallenberg.

Scene 3 NICHOLAS WRIGHT's rich writing for the RSC, the Royal Court and the National Theatre match his diverse theatrical experience and prompts him to bring Stanislavsky into the conversation, in the manner of Bulgakov.

Scene 4 RICHARD CURTIS' film and television comedies have included spoofing Shakespeare in the first series of *Blackadder* – here Chekhov extends his own gag.

Scene 5 TARIQ ALI started – consequently, he finishes. (*The Ballad of English Literature* is reproduced by kind permission of Terry Eagleton.)

We hope you enjoy this play. In buying a copy, you have made an extra contribution to The Gate's literary work. We can now look to the future with confidence, in the knowledge that we will be eternally grateful and indebted to nine very special and wonderfully supportive writers. Like all of The Gate's benefactors before them, they've done it out of the kindness of their hearts. But this time, a financial return will reward those efforts.

SIMON READE
Literary Manager
The Gate Theatre, Notting Hill
1991

ACT ONE

SCENE ONE

TARIQ ALI

The stage is bare except for a raised platform with a single throne-like chair. A host of US Senators and Congressmen/women enter talking excitedly to each other. Two of them – Congresswoman Jaqueline Tinker and Senator John Shulman – are in a state of advanced inebriety, leaning on each other as they whisper political obscenities. They are followed by a Professor in his seventies who is clearly not part of the crowd and takes a position at the front of the stage and looks wistfully at the audience before roaring with laughter. He sits on a chair. All freeze. A familiar tune is heard: "All Hail The Chief". Three tough security women enter. One plants the imperial eagle behind the chair. The other two take positions on either side. Silence.

SECURITY
WOMAN: Ladies and gentlemen. The President of the United States of America.

> *Musical flourish. The President enters. He is a tall, tough-looking black man in the uniform of a four-star General. He is greeted with polite applause by those present excluding the Professor.*

PRESIDENT: Happy Thanksgiving Day. *(Polite smiles.)* Time to talk turkey, eh? *(Laughs, but no one else joins him. Gets angry.)* Three years ago you told me to act tough. I turned them in. Locked them up. Got 'em off the streets. Put 'em behind bars. Act tough. And then what? This. We've lost our capital city.

SENATOR
SHULMAN: You blew it, asshole! Why do you think we put a black man in there. To sort out the garbage problem permanently. Instead . . . instead you screwed it up. If you'd sent in the Marines when it first started we'd have won. Now. Now . . . we need to bomb Washington. Clear the White House of those

motherfucking niggers. They've renamed it the Black House. What are we waiting for?

CONGRESS-
WOMAN
TINKER: Mr President. In order to save the White House we might have to destroy it.

PRESIDENT: Hey man, hey woman! Calm down there. Have you forgotten it was a mutiny in the Marines that started it all. I want to get back to Washington more than you. I hate being holed up here. I was to be the first black man in the White House. Remember?

ALL: *(Except Professor.)* Yeah! We remember!

PROFESSOR: *(Aside)* I can't believe it. I woke up today and didn't feel totally wiped out. A great morning.
It feels strange to be back on earth again.
Three years in space on a penal ship
For speaking my mind,
which they called treason.
With twenty others,
Survivors of the first wave,
Kept alive so that they have someone to negotiate with when peace is permitted to return.

It is the year two thousand and twenty-five;
The rulers of this country,
Those, that is, who are still alive,
Can't take it any more and
Are trying desperately to end this civil war now
But they don't know how.
That's why I've been released and brought down here.

PRESIDENT: Is the Professor here?

Security Women nod in unison.

SHULMAN: Mr President, I object. This man has justified the rebellions. He refuses to recant. I will not stay in the same room as him.

ANOTHER
SENATOR: Some of us find it difficult to stay in the same room as you, Senator Shulman, especially when there's no air conditioning. Your breath smells.

*Laughter from a few others. Professor is escorted by
Security Women before the President.*

PRESIDENT: Well Professor? What's the mood up there? Will they talk?

PROFESSOR: Not until they are released and brought back to earth. Then they wish to discuss terms of disengagement, but only after consulting their people.

THIRD
SENATOR: They're criminals who should be wiped out. Hell, Mr President, we've got to take a hard line if we're to preserve our next generation and future generations.

PROFESSOR: They are the future generations.

SHULMAN: Bullshit. Wipe them out!

TINKER: Every day I ask myself . . . I ask myself . . . Jaqueline, would you let your kids marry any of them? And I reply *(Screams)* NO! Shulman's talking sense, Mr President. Exterminate them.

PROFESSOR: You've tried and failed. You've killed thousands in LA and Chicago and eight hundred and twelve in Manhattan alone.

PRESIDENT: Correction, Professor. Eight hundred and eleven. Woody Allen had a heart attack.

PROFESSOR: *(Aside)* LA is still smouldering. The foot people – heard of them? – the FOOT people. Refugees who fled the killing fields of Central America on foot. Walked all the way to LA. Why? Because the gross national product of LA alone is higher than ninety percent of Latin America. That's why they came. The foot people. *(Chuckles)* They sure knew how to fight. The Chicanos were coming home to roost. Then the blacks joined the fray. The Marines mutinied. The Democrats panicked. Made a black General the President and, for good measure, flew in the Pope. LA, you see, is the largest Catholic congregation in the whole country. 300 parishes, 34,000 clerical and 12,000 lay employees. 275 elementary and 71 high schools. Nearly half a million students. Sounds good doesn't it, but the Pope hadn't been told that three-quarters of them were foot people. They didn't let the Pope enter LA. Instead they

demanded that all the Cardinals be sacked and ordinary
Catholics throughout the world be allowed to elect their
own Pope. This was blasphemy. *(Laughs)* They were
all excommunicated overnight. That's LA for you. It
was different in Chicago. A real civil war. Polish-
American vigilantes in and out of police uniforms and
the Irish versus the blacks. Then our friend here was
elected President. He thought he'd win over the blacks
by beating the shit out of the Polish-Americans.
Everyone united against the National Guard. Half the
city was burnt down. The rest was liberated. As for
New York. You won't believe it, but . . .

PRESIDENT: Professor? Er Professor! *(Professor turns.)* Listen,
Professor, these gangs of yours have killed off over half
the Senate and virtually the entire Congress. What you
see before you is the entire government of the United
States . . .

PROFESSOR: In exile . . .!

PRESIDENT: Sure, sure. All I was saying is that your side started the
killing.

PROFESSOR: My side didn't start anything. Not that I know what
my side is or what it wants. There are at least eight
sides in this dispute. Your problem is that the other
seven are all ranged against you, but none of them
started it off. You know that. Your capitalist quick-
buck juggernaut serves under twenty percent of the
population. The remaining eighty percent couldn't take
it any longer. So they stood up and said:

ALL: UP AGAINST THE WALL MOTHERFUCKERS!

PROFESSOR: Thank you.

PRESIDENT: I'm a General, Professor. I leave philosophy to the likes
of you. I'm offering you a pipe of peace. We'll release
the leaders of the rebellions as you demand. They will
be free to consult their people. But then we meet and
sort it out. But if those jerkoffs want to carry on this
mindless war then we'll finish them off. If it means
losing cities we shall do so in order to save America.
That includes Washington DC.

SHULMAN: Now you're talking!

ALL: *(Except Tinker.)* Shut the hell up!

                Enter a messenger who whispers to the President.

PRESIDENT: Professor, Senators. Excuse me for a few minutes.
                Special call in the secure facility. *(Exit)*

SHULMAN: Tell me something, Professor. What makes you tick,
                eh? *(Professor stares at him blankly.)* I mean what have
                you got up there. Why are your cells different from
                mine. We live in the same country, breathe the same
                air, talk the same language, belong to the same race.

ANOTHER
SENATOR: *(Winking at Tinker.)* Fuck in the same style.

A CONGRESS-
MAN: Surely you understand, Professor. I mean Shulman
                here is a pretty average-sized farmhouse pig. Well-
                reared, well-fed and well-fucked. *(President re-enters
                quietly and sits down.)* Why can't you be the same?
                Why, when he's on heat he spills his seed all over the
                shop. You ask the lift attendant at the Pentagon.

PRESIDENT: *(Grimly)* The disease is spreading. The Minneapolis
                farmers have declared Minnesota an independent
                Republic. The police and units of the National Guard
                have backed the farmers. I have talked to the Pentagon.
                We have no alternative but to sue for peace.

SHULMAN: *(Frothing)* I object, I tell you . . .

PRESIDENT: Quiet, you! They have denounced you and renounced
                you as their Senator. You are finished. Get out.

SHULMAN: I have been their standard-bearer for thirty years. I tell
                you . . .

PRESIDENT: Don't tell me! Tell them! There's a price on your head.
                Your house has been burnt down by angry neighbours.
                It's over for you. Now go. *(Exit Shulman.)* Professor. Is
                it true that you're directly descended from Buffalo Bill
                Cody?

PROFESSOR: *(Smiles and nods.)* Sure I am. My great-grandfather
                fought in the first Civil War against the Union. I'm
                just trying to correct his mistake.

PRESIDENT: Against a black President.

PROFESSOR : Capitalism is colour-blind, Mr President.

PRESIDENT : I have ordered the twenty prisoners to be landed on earth. They will touch down later today. I want direct talks between them and me tomorrow. Go and talk to them, Professor. We must stop this.

PROFESSOR : It need never have started. The demands were so simple. Now they want all of the cake and the baker's knife.

PRESIDENT : Professor. From your space prison you looked down on this earth, Professor. Did it look as fragile as it feels? Did you see storm-clouds when you were up there? *(Pause)* Tell them we are serious. I can't promise the whole cake. Why don't they accept half of it today? Otherwise this will not stop. They should be happy to behold me in a state of powerlessness. I have all the weaponry, all the arsenals are under my control, but you have strength. I understand that now. Let's make up and be friends. Will you tell them that?

PROFESSOR : I don't know. In our country it is very rare for the poor to defend themselves and win. If we have won the peace it is only because we dared to be seditious. For over two centuries now, those whom you defend have trampled over those who you want to talk to. The American dream? A joke. My friends up there feel that Watts must enter Malibu. Our country is heaven and hell in the same place, except that the citizens of Hell outnumber the denizens of Paradise by ten thousand to one! I will convey your message to the prisoners in outer space. I know what they'll ask me. *(Reflective)* Will injustice cease? Will starvation ever end?

ALL : NEVER! NEVER!

PRESIDENT : When THEY ask, I will reply, Professor. Now go and tell them that I am serious. This country must be saved. *(Exit Professor. Hubbub.)* Silence. My favourite adviser is History. *(Pauses)* Sometimes, in order to obtain victory it is necessary to let the other side believe that we have lost and they have won. This, then, becomes the basis of compromise and a new settlement. Of course, they who we have been fighting for three years, are not fools. When they feel settled,

truly settled, they will realise one day that they have
been defeated. This will make them angry but they will
realise their powerlessness. Some of them, you see, will
feel more settled than others. It is a simple plan, but it
always works. *(Pause)* Please go and rest. Tomorrow
night we will meet again and I will report on the peace
talks. God Bless America. *(All applaud and exit.*
President walks up and down in deep thought, then he
smiles. The smile gets wider. He grins. And sings:)
There were three four-star Generals
Set out to win this war.
The first got shot in Chicago
The second became unsure.
I became the President
Pledged to crush them all.
And I will have my victory,
They the victory ball.
We'll all have peace and friendship
Unless . . . *(Frowns)*
Unless it all goes wrong!
Poor song!

SCENE TWO

RANJIT BOLT

As the President concludes his song, Mrs Thatcher, now a bent and
wizened figure, dressed in Queen Victoria costume is carried in on a litter
borne by four massive Nubian slaves. Attached to the litter, clearly visible
to the audience, is a banner with the caption: "1925 – 2025" emblazoned
on it. The Nubians set her down, centre stage and she addresses the
President.

THATCHER: Hail, dusky tenant of the seat of power!
            You sought our aid in this, your darkest hour:
            Behold! Responding to your call, we come,
            Leaving the comfort of our Barratt home,
            Reluctantly transporting, with great pain,
            Our withered carcass on an aeroplane

Across the salt wastes of th' Atlantic main.
Dulwich's Sybil, we – Thatcher our name –
A mighty leader of immortal fame;
The counsellor of presidents and sheikhs,
Long since forgiven for our own mistakes;
All the world's heads of state seek our advice:
In politics, brief absence will suffice
To cleanse a leader's sins. Ours was the fate
Of Richard Nixon after Watergate –
Scorned for a year – for decades wined and dined;
A fiend in power, a saint when we'd resigned.
All Britain loathed us once, but now we're fêted –
Our hundredth birthday's being celebrated
This very week . . .
(She breaks off suddenly and indulges in brief, paranoid
speculation.)
                              Unless they want our death –
Blowing the candles out with our last breath. . .?
(She recovers her composure.)
But no: the frailer we appear, the more we are
Admired and loved, like Queen Victoria!
IT'S A FUNNY OLD WORLD! And its applause
Comes, goes, returns, from no apparent cause:
We thought we could go on and on and on –
Instead of doing that, we've simply gone!
Once we had been so rash as to describe,
In that unfortunate psittaceous jibe,
The death of Liberal Democracy,
Power slipped, with treacherous alacrity,
Out of our grasp! Be resolute! BE STRONG!!
Then must your reign be prosperous and long.
Yes! Massacre those clapped-out ideologues
And throw their bodies to the White House dogs!
Above all, there must be NO TURNING BACK –
Turn it and you'll be stabbed in it! ATTACK!
Recall my slip with Heseltine and Howe –
Launch a pre-emptive strike and launch it now!
These whingeing radicals are out of date –
They had their chance in 1968 –
They didn't take it and the tide soon turned –
This is a lesson that they should have learned.
Invite them to the conference table, yes –
But kill them there! That'll sort out this mess!

An Officer enters.

OFFICER: Riots in Watts. They've marched on Malibu!

PRESIDENT: Quell them at once! SHOOT TO KILL!

Exit Officer.

THATCHER: Good for you!
Show Watts what's what!
(She pauses, evidently weary now.)
                                     It's time for us to go –
Our plane is waiting.

PRESIDENT: I'd just like to know
One thing. . . .

THATCHER: Go on. . . .

PRESIDENT: Everyone loathed you.

THATCHER: True.
(A pause.)
Well? What about it?

PRESIDENT: Did it worry you?

The wizened figure, now once again borne aloft on its litter, does not respond, but simply laughs, softly at first, but rising steadily to a crescendo that echoes the Professor's laughter at the start of the play. Exit Thatcher.

The Messenger from Scene One now re-enters.

MESSENGER: The delegates are ready to begin, Mr President.

PRESIDENT: You'd better show them in.
(The Messenger goes out.)
Uneasy lies the head that wears the crown:
I'll have to gun these fucking pinkoes down!
(The Messenger returns, followed by the Professor and ten delegates of sundry ilks and hues. He gestures to the conference table and they take their seats, squabbling amongst themselves about the "placement". The Professor remains aloof from this unpleasantness, seating himself, anyhow, once it has subsided. Meanwhile, unseen by any of them, the President has hastily whispered his instructions to the Messenger, who exits, smiling, with a quick, significant glance at the Delegates. The President

now opens the proceedings. He seems hesitant in addressing
the Delegates.)
Gentlemen; ladies – ladies; gentlemen . . .
(Pause)
Shit!
(Gets it right at last:)
       GENTLEPERSONS! So – we meet again.
I can recall your faces to a man. . . .
Shit! PERSON! . . . from the day when this began –
When you demanded that the White House be
Renamed – although you couldn't quite agree
The colour, seeing all your different shades.
It's called the Black House now: it's full of spades.
Satisfied? But I take it your demands
This time contain a little more substance?

> *The Spokesperson, a Hispanic woman, now rises and*
> *reads from a paper. She delivers the first sentence in*
> *an aggressively perfunctory tone.*

SPOKES-
PERSON: May all the world re-echo with your praise,
Mr President. Right. Our demands: the gays
Want an enormous monument put up
In downtown DC to Professor Krupp.

PRESIDENT: *(Explanatory, to audience:)*
Professor Krupp – the man who found a cure
For AIDS.

SPOKES-
PERSON: What answer can I give them?

PRESIDENT: Sure.

SPOKES-
PERSON: Good. Here are the designs.

> *The President is still standing. He reaches over, takes*
> *the plans, and hands them to an aide, who must have*
> *entered at some point during the above.*

PRESIDENT: Anything more?

IRISH
AMERICAN
DELEGATE: Jesus! You think that's all we came here for?
Some faggot phallic symbol! What the fuck . . .?

GAY
DELEGATE: Illiterate fascist!

IRISH
AMERICAN
DELEGATE: Hey! Don't push yer luck!

The Irish American Delegate and the Gay Delegate are about to come to blows when the President raises a restraining hand.

PRESIDENT: Control yourselves! Please! You're all guests of mine.

He gestures to the Spokesperson to proceed.

SPOKES-
PERSON: The sick and dying want free healthcare.

PRESIDENT: Fine.

SPOKES-
PERSON: The young demand state-funded education.
(President nods consent.)
The hard-line feminists want menstruation
Abolished.

PRESIDENT: Fine by me.

SPOKES-
PERSON: The students need . . .
(She squints at the paper.)
They've written it themselves – it's hard to read . . .
"An end to the requirement, . . ."

PRESIDENT: Allow me.
(He takes the paper from her brusquely and reads:)
". . . to the requirement for literacy."!
You sure they mean that?

Hands back the paper.

SPOKES-
PERSON: It appears they do.
And they're against lectures and study, too!

PRESIDENT: OK. What's next?

The Professor has grown increasingly angry during these exchanges. He now interrupts, addressing the President.

PROFESSOR: Wait! Are you saying you
                Agree to all of our demands so far?

PRESIDENT: Correct.

DELEGATE 1:   Fuck!

DELEGATE 2:   Shit!

DELEGATE 3:   It's fascist!

DELEGATE 4:   Worse: bourgeois!

PRESIDENT: *(Mockingly)* No harm intended!

PROFESSOR: MISTER President!
                You're well aware this isn't what we meant –
                Not what we meant at all. The People rise
                To FIGHT. Get tough!

PRESIDENT: Well! I apologise.
                OK: the gays can't have their monument.

GAY
DELEGATE: This is an outrage!

                *He attempts to leave, but his path is blocked by one of
                the Marines who have silently begun entering.*

PRESIDENT: *(More mockery.)* OK – I relent!

                He holds up his arms in mock surrender.

PROFESSOR: This is preposterous!

PRESIDENT: What am I to do?
                Whichever hand I play, I lose!

DELEGATE 6:   That's true –
                He's got a point, you guys. . . .

DELEGATE 7:   Schmuck! Who asked you?

                *Delegate 7 proceeds to throttle Delegate 6. The
                Marines are ready to intervene, but the President
                discourages them with a slight shake of the head. All
                this is still unnoticed by the Delegates, who are in
                indignant uproar, squabbling among themselves.*

PRESIDENT: Delegates! Please! You won't do any good
                Squabbling and spilling one another's blood.
                I think I've found the ultimate solution. . . .

PROFESSOR: What, Mr President?

PRESIDENT: Mass execution!

*He gives a signal, whereupon the Marines open fire,
gunning down the remaining nine delegates.
Meanwhile, two Marines arrest the Professor.*

SCENE THREE

ADRIAN MITCHELL

*The Amazonian Desert. Night. The Army of the Dead enter, slowly.
They lay down a yellow cloth shaped like the northern half of South
America.*

SOLDIER
ONE: This is the Amazonian Desert.

*Soldiers place on the Desert a campfire. It burns cold
and blue. The Soldiers sit around it. They are men
and women, more women than men, and maybe a few
children. They wear baggy combat fatigues. Their
helmets are like skulls, but we can see their faces. All
their faces are marked with scarlet burns.*

SOLDIER
TWO: We are the Army of the Dead.

SOLDIER
ONE: Most nights we sit under the Brazilian moon, getting
            drunk on the oil we suck from the wreckage of
            Japanese tanks.

SOLDIER
THREE: To pass the time, we tell each other stories about the
            old days when we were alive.

SOLDIER
FOUR: I was standing in the library and she was passing by
            and her breast just brushed against my shoulder.

*Other Soldiers nod and smile, appreciating the story
quietly, both men and women.*

SOLDIER
FIVE:

I was stationed in Edinburgh before the Burning and I was packing my kit to go on leave and one of the other squaddies took a trombone out of his locker and he sat on his bed and began to play a slow blues. And my heart filled up like a mug of beer.

SOLDIER
SIX:

My boyfriend and I went for a ride in a hot air balloon and it was springtime and a wind rose up so we lost as much height as we could and we found ourselves clutching the rim of the basket as we were dragged through an apple orchard in full blossom and all we could see was pink and white and all we could hear was our own laughter and the hot air roaring like a hollow lion.

SOLDIER
TWO:

I remember.

SOLDIER
SIX:

You weren't in the basket.

SOLDIER
TWO:

Nope. I was in one of the apple trees.

SOLDIER
THREE:

Yes, we tell stories about peacetime.

SOLDIER
TWO:

They pass the time while we're waiting for new recruits to the Army of the Dead, somewhere in the Amazonian Desert.

> *Enter Soldiers Seven and Eight carrying a stretcher. On it is Soldier Nine. He is just about breathing. They put down his stretcher. Other Soldiers gather to look at him knowledgably, but keeping their distance.*

SOLDIER
SEVEN:

New recruit, lads.

SOLDIER
ONE:

What's his name?

SOLDIER
EIGHT:

Hasn't been able to talk to us yet. He's still alive.

SOLDIER SEVEN:	He's going.

Soldiers echo the last breaths and death rattle of Soldier Nine. Soldier Nine dies.

SOLDIER TWO:	You're good and dead now. You can get up.

Soldier Nine climbs sleepily out of his stretcher, stands up. He is a burned man.

SOLDIER ONE:	What's your name, then?

SOLDIER NINE:	Corporal Alex Ferguson.

SOLDIER TWO:	You can drop the Corporal. No ranks in the Army of the Dead.

SOLDIER THREE:	*(Interested)* How did you cop it?

SOLDIER
NINE:

Ten holes. They gave me ten. Ten holes.

★Two holes were the size of the holes in my ears.
They were rounded, and as they opened and shut
They seemed to make a sound like sighing.

Two holes were the size of my nostrils,
Close together and dark inside
And breathing out a smell of something – rotting.

Two holes were the size of my eyes
And they were trying to clench themselves
To hold back – the red tears.

One hole was the size of my mouth
And it cried out
With the voice of – an old child.

One hole was the size of the hole
In the end of my cock
And it was skewered by a white-hot, turning gimlet.

One hole was the size of the hole in my arse,

★*(Note: this could be sung to a bluesy, irregular, simple sort of tune if anyone can set it.)*

Small and wincing away from the light.
And it went – very deep.

Petrol was poured into all my holes.
All of my holes were set on fire.

They covered my holes with a clean uniform.
They flew me home. There was a flag.
In the village I loved, they put me in a hole.

SOLDIER
THREE: Is there any pain left?

SOLDIER
NINE: I still hate the living. That hurts.

SOLDIER
THREE: That'll go away.

SOLDIER
TEN: I still feel it sometimes.

SOLDIER
TWO: Oh you feel a bloody sight too much.

SOLDIER
NINE: Who are you?

SOLDIER
THREE: Don't ask him.

SOLDIER
TWO: He's only Samuel Taylor Coleridge.

SOLDIER
TEN: (*Who is Samuel Taylor Coleridge, burly, energetic.)
                The English living haven't changed in two hundred
                and thirty years.

SOLDIER
ONE: Hit it, Sam.

SOLDIER
TEN: Secure from actual warfare, we have loved
                To swell the war-whoop, passionate for war!
                Alas! for ages ignorant of all
                Its ghastlier workings (famine or blue plague,
                Battle, or siege, or flight through wintry snows),
                We, this whole people, have been clamorous
                For war and bloodshed; animating sports

*(Note: Simon Callow as Coleridge if possible.)

The which we pay for as a thing to talk of,
Spectators and not combatants! No guess
Anticipative of a wrong unfelt,
No speculation on contingency,
However dim and vague, too vague and dim
To yield a justifying cause; and forth,
(Stuffed out with big preamble, holy names,
And adjurations of the God in Heaven),
We send our mandates for the certain deaths
Of thousands and ten thousands! Boys and girls
And women, that would groan to see a child
Pull off an insect's leg, all read of war,
The best amusement for our morning meal!
The poor wretch, who has learnt his only prayers
From curses, who knows scarcely words enough
To ask a blessing from his Heavenly Father,
Becomes a fluent phraseman, absolute
And technical in victories and defeats,
And all our dainty terms for fratricide;
Terms which we trundle smoothly o'er our tongues
Like mere abstractions, empty sounds to which
We join no feeling and attach no form!
As if the soldier died without a wound;
As if the fibres of this godlike frame
Were gored without a pang; as if the wretch
Who fell in battle, doing bloody deeds,
Passed off to Heaven, translated and not killed;
As though he had no wife to pine for him,
No God to judge him! Therefore, evil days
Are coming on us, O my countrymen!
And what if all-avenging Providence
Strong and retributive, should make us know
The meaning of our words, force us to feel
The desolation and the agony
Of our fierce doings?*

> *Other Soldiers have followed Coleridge's speech closely, encouraging him quietly.*

SOLDIER
NINE: What can we do?

*(Note: this is from Coleridge's Fears In Solitude, written in 1798.)

SOLDIER
ONE: Too late for us to do much.

SOLDIER
TWO: We can sing.

SOLDIERS
ONE AND
TWO: *(Sing)*
                Once upon a time
                There was a mighty forest
                It stretched all the way
                From Mexico down to Cape Horn.
                But the human race
                Brought axes and saws
                Year after year
                Century by century
                And branch by branch
                And tree by tree
                That mighty forest was reduced
                To a desert of murderous sand.

ALL
SOLDIERS: *(Sing)*
                Took a long time
                Took a long long time
                But they cut them all down in the end
                Took a long time
                Took a long long time
                But they cut them all down in the end.

SOLDIERS
ONE AND
TWO: *(Sing)*
                Once upon a time
                I knew a man and woman
                And every year
                They planted a hundred odd trees.
                And their seven kids
                Keep planting those trees
                Year after year
                Century by century
                And branch by branch
                And tree by tree

That mighty forest will return
And the creatures will sing its shade.

ALL
SOLDIERS: *(Sing)*
Takes a long time
Takes a long long time
But the trees will return in the end
Takes a long time
Takes a long long time
But peace will prevail in the end.
Takes a long time
Takes a long long time
But peace will prevail in the end.

> *Enter Messenger from previous scenes, now in smart
> new Army uniform, carrying a modern rifle.*

MESSENGER: *(To audience.)* Got my call-up papers. Got yours yet?
Nobody's told me why I'm here, or what the war's
about.

SOLDIER
TWO: It's about time somebody did.

SOLDIER
ONE: Hang around and listen, kid.

SOLDIER
FOUR: *(Sings)*
*And once again the politicians
Whose greatest talent is for lying
Are sending you where they're afraid to go
To do their killing and dying.

You're young, and you've been trained to fight,
You're brave, well-equipped and loyal.
That's why they're sending you to Hell –
    Blood and Oil.

ALL
SOLDIERS: *(Sing)*
You're young, and you've been trained to fight,
You're brave, well-equipped and loyal.
That's why they're sending you to Hell –
    Blood and Oil.

*(Note: this has been set to music by Peter Moser.)

SOLDIER
FOUR: *(Sings)*
It's not to defend the Falklands' sheep
Or keep Christians apart in Ireland,
But to sit in a tank till you are cooked
In a giant oven of desert sand.

You're not here to fight against tyranny
Or for hostages or British soil,
But for economics, the dollars of death –
    Blood and Oil.

ALL
SOLDIERS: *(Sing)*
You're not here to fight against tyranny
Or for hostages or British soil
But for economics, the dollars of death –
    Blood and Oil.

SOLDIER
FOUR: *(Sings)*
And the soldiers you fight will be young men
With no reason to kill young men like you,
With beautiful families back home
And some with wives and children too.

But no politicians will be there
When lungs tear and arteries boil –
They'll be filmed with survivors in hospital –
    Blood and Oil.

ALL
SOLDIERS: *(Sing)*
But no politicians will be there
When lungs tear and arteries boil.
They'll be filmed with survivors in hospital –
    Blood and Oil.

SOLDIER
FOUR: *(Sings)*
Yes, once again the politicians
Whose greatest talent is for lying
Are sending young men where old men dare not go
To do their killing and dying

ALL
SOLDIERS: *(Sing)*
    To do their killing and dying
    To do their killing and dying
    To do their killing and dying –

SOLDIER
FOUR: *(Sings)*
    Blood and Oil.

ALL
SOLDIERS: *(Sing)*
    Blood and Oil
    Blood and Oil
    Blood and Oil
    Blood and Oil.

The Army of the Dead pick up their desert and their campfire in a burst of light. They exit.

SCENE FOUR

MICHAEL MEYER

The President's private apartment. The President at his desk.

PRESIDENT: *(Murmurs to himself as he consults handwritten notes.)*
The gross national product of LA alone is higher than ninety per cent of Latin America . . . Polish vigilantes . . . Irish versus the Blacks . . . Clear the White House of those motherfucking niggers . . . Lift attendant at the Pentagon . . . *(There is a knock at the door.)* Come in.

The First Lady enters.

FIRST LADY: May I – ?

PRESIDENT: In a moment. Dulwitch's Sybil. Dulwitch's Sybil? Do we know anyone called Sybil Dulwitch?

FIRST LADY: Not that I recall.

PRESIDENT: Maybe a town called Dulwitch?

FIRST LADY: I think there's one in Vermont.

PRESIDENT: There are some funny people in Vermont.

FIRST LADY: There are some funny people in Washington.

PRESIDENT: That's for sure. So what can I do for you?
Housekeeping money, I suppose?

FIRST LADY: What do you mean, housekeeping money? Something
wrong with our credit?

PRESIDENT: No, no. At least, I hope not.

FIRST LADY: Are you feeling OK?

PRESIDENT: Yeah. It was just a line in a play I remembered.

FIRST LADY: Maybe you should see a doctor.

PRESIDENT: Ah, that's what you'd like.

FIRST LADY: Anyway you ain't seen a play in years.

PRESIDENT: I saw it on the box.

FIRST LADY: A play on the box? You must be kidding.

PRESIDENT: When I was in Europe. It was by some Swedish guy.
How is Bertha?

FIRST LADY: Bertha who?

PRESIDENT: Have you forgotten our daughter's name?

FIRST LADY: Our daughter happens to be called Martha.

PRESIDENT: Yes, yes, I mean Martha. The daughter in this play was
called Bertha. *(Suddenly, violently.)* Who is her father?

FIRST LADY: How can I tell?

PRESIDENT: Then you admit being unfaithful?

FIRST LADY: What's my fidelity to do with it? I haven't read the
fucking play.

PRESIDENT: But you haven't denied being unfaithful.

Martha, sixteen, enters.

MARTHA: Hi, pop. Hi, ma. *(Pause)* Anything wrong?

FIRST LADY: Your father's a little confused this morning.

MARTHA: I'm not surprised. All those blacks in the White House.

FIRST LADY: No, it's some European play he's been watching.

MARTHA: You taken to watching plays, pop? That's great.

FIRST LADY: He thinks he ain't your father.

MARTHA: Ain't you, pop?

PRESIDENT: You should address that question to your mother.

MARTHA: Ain't he, ma?

FIRST LADY: Unfortunately, yes.

PRESIDENT: The nurse knows the truth.

The First Lady and Martha stare at him.

MARTHA: What nurse, pop?

PRESIDENT: Yours, of course. And mine. *(The First Lady and Martha exchange a glance.)* Why was Bertha – Martha – not born until three years after our marriage?

FIRST LADY: Hank, she was born eight months after we married.

PRESIDENT: There you are! Eight months!

FIRST LADY: By Caesarian, for Christ's sake.

PRESIDENT: Wait a minute, wait a minute. That month before our marriage. You went to West Virginia.

FIRST LADY: To tell my ma.

PRESIDENT: To tell her, yes. But you didn't tell me.

FIRST LADY: *(Patiently)* I went to tell her you and I were getting married.

PRESIDENT: *(Speaks remembered words.)* Suppose you were prepared for anything rather than lose your child? Suppose you were telling me the truth now when you said: 'Bertha is my child, not yours.' My power over her would be ended. *(Cries)* Harness the sleigh! *(Puts his hands to his head.)* The nurse knows the truth.

The First Lady and Martha exchange another glance.

FIRST LADY: Maybe you'd better get the nurse, Martha.

MARTHA: *(Sadly)* I guess so. *(Goes)*

FIRST LADY: Hank, why don't you take one of those green pills
Doctor Eagleberger prescribed for you when you get
upset?

PRESIDENT: Ah, Doctor Eagleberger. Yes, he's got horns, too. No, I
know what those pills contain.

FIRST LADY: At least let me get you a glass of water.

PRESIDENT: *(Cunningly)* One can't trust what comes out of the tap
nowadays.

FIRST LADY: We've got bottled water.

PRESIDENT: But who filled the bottle? Why is Martha taking so
long?

FIRST LADY: I think I hear the lift.

PRESIDENT: The lift attendant at the Pentagon. We know what he
saw. *(Martha enters with a strapping female Nurse.)* Ah,
Margaret, you're the only friend I have. You've been
like a mother to me.

NURSE: That's right, Mr President. I'm your friend.

PRESIDENT: You've seen it all from the beginning. A web is being
spun around me here. There's no one here who loves
me except you. *(Pause)* Is it true that if you cross a
zebra with a horse, you get striped foals?

NURSE: *(Gently)* Quite true, Mr President.

PRESIDENT: Is it also true that if you cross the same mare with an
ordinary stallion, the foals may continue to be striped?

NURSE: I guess so.

PRESIDENT: Then a brown stallion can sire a striped foal. *Ergo*, it
can never be proved who is a child's father. *(Pause)*
Someone has been intercepting my letters. *(Looks round
and picks up a lamp from the desk.)* This is no use.

NURSE: Why not, Mr President?

PRESIDENT: It contains no oil. If I throw it, it will not catch fire.

NURSE: Mr President, you're tired. Why don't you have a nice
sleep?

PRESIDENT: The Iraqis are behind this. Or can it be those Polish

immigrants? Or Dulwitch Sybil? Yes, I am terribly
tired.

NURSE: Why don't you let me put you to bed on the sofa here?
I'll just get something to keep you warm. *(Goes)*

PRESIDENT: *(To First Lady.)* She's the only one who understands
me. This morning I went to the post office –

FIRST LADY: Went to the post office?

PRESIDENT: And collected my letters before you could intercept
them. It is evident from them that you have been
destroying both my outgoing and my incoming
correspondence. The resultant waste of time has
virtually destroyed the value of my researches.

MARTHA: What researches, pop?

PRESIDENT: My scientific researches, of course. A man in Barcelona
has been working along the same lines and may arrive
at his conclusions before I do. Your mother – *(Bitterly)*
– yes, *your* mother, of that there can be no doubt – has
moreover been turning my former friends against me
by spreading a rumour concerning my sanity. That is
why the Russians have become cool lately. *(The Nurse
returns with a straitjacket.)* Mrs Thatcher would have
known what to do. What have you got there, Margaret?
(Puzzled) Didn't we all call you Maggie once?

NURSE: A nice dressing-gown to keep you warm, Mr President.

PRESIDENT: Oh, Maggie, you're the only one who understands me.
You've always understood the men who live in this
house. *(Remembers)* But this isn't the White House,
that's full of blacks. Can you really be a woman?

NURSE: *(Bridles)* Say, don't you – ! *(Controls herself.)* 'Course
I'm a woman, Mr President.

PRESIDENT: But you're so gentle and kind. That dressing-gown
looks too big for me.

NURSE: It'll fit you nicely. Now just you stretch out your arms
so I can put it on you. *(The President stretches out his
arms meekly. The Nurse puts them into the straitjacket.)*
That's a good boy. Now turn round.

PRESIDENT: *(As she ties the straps at the back.)* Do you remember,

Margaret – Maggie – when I was your dear little baby, how you used to tuck me up at night and say my prayers with me? And how you lit the candle and told me pretty stories when I had bad dreams and couldn't sleep? Do you remember?

NURSE: Sure, I remember.

PRESIDENT: And how once I took the big carving-knife and wanted to make boats, and you had to get the knife away from me by telling me a story?

NURSE: We had to tell you stories because you thought we all wanted to hurt you. Give me that snake, I said, otherwise he'll bite you. And you let go of the knife. *(She has fastened the straitjacket.)* Now it's time to go to bed. *(Tries to guide him towards the sofa.)*

PRESIDENT: What's that, Maggie? Must I go to bed when I'm dressed? *(Realizes his situation.)* Damnation! Oh, you damned woman! Who could have believed you could be so cunning? Oh, Maggie. You would never have done this to Ronald Reagan. Dulwitch Sybil! Of course! Yes, you were close with that Gorbachev. You have all conspired against me. Was Gorby a woman too? *(Cries)* Get those blacks out of the White House! *(Tries to spit at the First Lady, but shudders and falls still.)*

FIRST LADY: Oh, Hank! There won't be any more blacks in the White House for a long time now.

MARTHA: Couldn't you take over, ma?

Pause.

FIRST LADY: Mebbe I could, Martha. Yea. Mebbe I could.

SCENE FIVE

NICK DEAR

FIRST LADY: I don't get it. My husband flies to Europe for a summit, sees a play on TV there, and promptly goes insane. Previously he was a fine upstanding American

with mild psychopathic tendencies – the ultimate
quarterback. Now he's in the Barbara Bush Home for
Personalities With Problems. What was the thing he
saw that could have such potency? What is a play,
anyway? Art, what is it? I know in my bones but I just
can't remember. Now that I've made peace with all our
warring factions, I think we need some of that stuff
they have in Europe, right here by our own firesides. I
have put our greatest minds to work on the subject, but
they've all drawn a blank. They say: how do you create
culture from zilch? In despair I turn to the occupants of
our deepest, oldest dungeons . . . Martha, wheel him in!
(Martha enters sheepishly.) Well? Where's the Professor? Is
he, ah, *(Improvising)* finishing off that new theorem he's
been working on during his, ah, period of captivity? –
Martha, answer me!

MARTHA: I'm very sorry but I don't feel I can go on. What you
             were saying – it's got me thinking.

FIRST LADY: *(Alarmed)* Thinking? Why?

MARTHA: I just don't want to be associated with this. I find it
             puerile, silly, witless and crass. It's not only my career,
             although – well you know what I mean – there could
             be casting people *(Gestures 'out there'.)* I've enjoyed
             being the President's spoilt little girl, really I have, but
             this futuristic piss-take in American accents is just
             juvenile, isn't it? Juvenile, isn't that the word? I mean
             I know it's not my place to make value-judgements –
             heavens, I only just got my card, playing the chemist in
             'What? No Condoms!' at Pitlochry – but who honestly
             wants to hear about Mrs Thatcher any more? I mean
             who cares what kind of wretched house she lives in?

             The Professor enters, unguarded.

PROFESSOR: Martha, stick to the script!

MARTHA: Script? You call this a script? I've seen better scripts in
             a Christmas cracker. You get more plot in a cornflakes
             ad. And as for global politics – Noddy and bloody Big
             Ears have an infinitely wider perspective than this lot!

FIRST LADY: It's in a good cause, though, dear.

MARTHA: Is it? What's the purpose of it, then?

FIRST LADY: Well, to help to keep our theatres open.

MARTHA: Why? So they can put on a load of fourth-form humour, interspersed with little ditties telling you the same thing eighteen times over to a tune that sounds like seals being culled? I'd rather go down the video shop, and at least be entertained!

PROFESSOR: Martha, this is only meant to be a bit of a laugh. Have a giggle, raise a few bob. You're the wrong generation to be taking everything so seriously – that's my generation, that's the author's generation, you're supposed to be young and fucking carefree, so where have the fucking scruples come from all of a fucking sudden? Get on with the show!

MARTHA: Why?

FIRST LADY: Because a show is a thing you get on with!

MARTHA: But if it's *bad*, should we do it? This stuff is bad. It's not good art. What kind of advertisement for the theatre is this? A play should have characters, plot, excitement, be about something, shouldn't it? All the plays I like are about something. Why junk all that? It's not reactionary to junk all that, it's just lazy. This will simply fade away . . . It'll die out because nobody's interested, not from lack of subsidy, but because nobody could give a toss about the dull, indulgent charades of these dull, indulgent people. We've all got better things to do. And it's racist. I'm not being funny, it is. "Oh, here's an American, he must be stupid". I'm not being clever. But Christ!

PROFESSOR: Martha, you've really lowered the tone.

FIRST LADY: I must say, I'm a little confused about the Amazonian desert.

PROFESSOR: People feel things very deeply, they feel the way the US behaves in the world is disgusting, they want to blow off steam. A piece like this is a perfectly good vehicle for blowing off steam. You can't deny that anger. It's real.

FIRST LADY: And Samuel Taylor Coleridge was a very angry poet. Everybody says.

PROFESSOR: Now let's get back to it. Pick up from my cue: "Yes, First Lady, I was in London. Before the First Oil War, when – "

MARTHA: No!

PROFESSOR: Look, swallow your pride, you stupid girl! Where's the harm?

MARTHA: I won't!

FIRST LADY: Just do the scene for me, sweetheart, and I'll take you to Orso's for supper.

MARTHA: No! I don't want to go to Orso's!

FIRST LADY: She don't want to go to Orso's . . . *(A gesture: 'What can you do?')*

MARTHA: I just think we have to try harder!

FIRST LADY: Ah, shit.

MARTHA: *(Turns to audience.)* Ladies and gentlemen –

PROFESSOR: Oh, leave them out of it.

MARTHA: Ladies and gentlemen, I'm embarrassed that you've had to sit through –

FIRST LADY: Are you kidding? I've been giving my all!

MARTHA: And I want to apologise for the general low standard of –

PROFESSOR: *(To audience.)* Is this what they teach at RADA nowadays? Involving the audience? Breaking down the Fourth Wall? Awfully old hat, Martha love, we were doing all this when you were still combing your pigtails. Once Peter Brook asked me to go down into the stalls at the Aldwych and –

MARTHA: *(Angry)* I'm not interested! – Ladies and gentlemen, I'm going to begin a new story straight after the interval, which will tell things the proper way, the true way – please watch my show, don't watch this! Let them carry on with their old ranting and raving about left and right, their clever-clever hypotheses and bash-the-rich cartoons – I'll tell you something about *life*.

FIRST LADY: Your agent will have kittens.

MARTHA: I don't care!

PROFESSOR: You'll be on your own. It's cold out there . . .

MARTHA: *(Now apprehensive.)* I'll risk it.

> *Enter the four Nubian Slaves.*

SLAVES: We're with Martha! We also think it stinks! We always get cast as Nubian slaves and we're not gonna take it any more!

FIRST LADY: Professor, you're the only hope!

PROFESSOR: Yes, First Lady, I was in London. Before the First Oil War, when the West End was aglow with the lights of many a Temple of Art. Why, in those days you could do anything, anything you wanted: historical shows, biblical shows, animal shows – as long as you did it to *music*.

MARTHA: More of the same! Cheap jibes at the musical form, just because the wanker who wrote this can't do it!

SLAVES: Let's get to work, Martha!

MARTHA: Right! – We shall return.

> *Exit Martha and the Slaves.*

FIRST LADY: I don't know about you, Professor, but Jesus Christ, I need a drink.

> *Blackout.*

END OF ACT ONE

ACT TWO

SCENE ONE

ARNOLD WESKER

Empty stage. No stage lights. House lights up. The actress who was Martha enters. Chastened. We must now call her Actress.

ACTRESS: We have a problem. I speak for author six: it is not easy to continue. What you are about to witness is the author using an actress to make sense of his thoughts. And he's *telling* you that this is happening. He's even telling you that he's telling you! Here is the problem: the last author broke down the fourth wall and criticised the work of His/Her colleagues. More: He/She promised to begin – I quote: ". . . a new story straight after the interval which will tell things the proper way, the true way . . . something about *life* . . ." Well, it *is* after the interval but He/She has fled! He/She is not here to tell you 'a new story . . . theproperwaythetrueway . . . about *life* . . .' with, presumably, a capital 'L'. He/She has left it to me. And although He/She may be in possession and full command of 'theproperwaythetrueway' *I* – am not! What am I – speaking as the author – left with? What are my options? I could invent a little scene about four black men and a white woman and have the actors perform it; I could sketch an idea and let them improvise each night; I could ignore the colleague before me who exploded everything and go back to a scene or character from one of the other scenes to pick up where they left off; or I could just talk to you about what has happened and see where it leads. My instinct is to begin with the last option. Just talk. Your last author chucked everything out of the window and said 'let's start again'. I can't ignore that. If you have been engaged by the previous scenes then the illusion has by now been broken for you. You must be quite distressed, irritated. I'm sorry. It's not my fault. I'm left to pick up the pieces. It's not easy –

The next passage is the Author's Voice Over on tape, speaking while Actress mouths the words.

AUTHOR
V.O.:   – especially as it's not me you are hearing but an actress who is mouthing words for me.

Pause. Actress opens and closes her mouth attempting to say something. Nothing comes out. She seems tongue-tied, speechless, makes only choking sounds. Terror enters her eyes as though she's gripped by an outside force, as though she's programmed. She continues silently to mouth the Author's words, deeply distressed. Tears if possible.

(Continuing) Disconcerting, isn't it! Even distressing. Here I am, quietly talking to you on tape which is being played back to you while the actress who is speaking for me, or rather is supposed to be speaking for me, is not! She's simply moving her lips to synchronise with my voice. Observe how distressed, even terrified, she is, as though gripped by an outside force and powerless to do anything about it.

Hold the terror. Then – Actress changes to her pleasant self. In control. Which is what actors are trained to do – move from mood to mood in a flash. It is her voice from here on.

ACTRESS: But observe, too, how quickly she can change. Oh, not instantly, of course not, she requires a little time to control herself but look – a few seconds pause, a few blows into her handkerchief and – presto! She can talk calmly. *(Beat)* I can talk calmly. *(Beat)* Or is it *she* can talk calmly? *(Beat)* So dangerous, drama. So easy to manipulate an audience. Manipulate their emotion, their thinking. 'Manipulate' is an emotive word, isn't it? Carries with it the sense of making you feel intensely or think urgently that which is not honest, or that which is superficial and without substance. Nor is it *that* simple, since all art can be viewed as a form of manipulation. Distinctions must be made, between manipulating you to feel that which is not honest, and manipulating you to feel that which you may not want to feel. The former – to make you feel that which is not

honest – is unacceptable. The latter – to make you feel
that which you may not want to feel – is legitimate.
And what makes it difficult for you, the audience, to
distinguish between what is dishonest but attractive,
and what is honest but difficult-to-swallow, is that both
use the dangerously potent elements of theatre. Namely
– lights –

House lights go down, slowly, slowly. Dramatic
lighting on stage focuses upon a central area. Music:
Terje Rypdal's Ineo Op. 29 (CD ECM 1389). Four
black actors enter. Three tenderly carry a fourth who
is 'dead'. Actress slowly merges into character. She is
the 'dead man's' wife. She is distraught. Moves to help
lower the body to the ground. She kneels by to grieve.
Her grief is deep and disturbing. The three step back.
One by one they turn to look off-stage in the direction
where, we assume, the awful deed took place. Creeping
over the music is the sound, barely audible but
unmistakable, of a crowd cheering. One of the three
rushes towards the sound as though about to wreak
vengeance. The other two restrain him. On this tableau
– dead man, grieving wife, angry companion,
restraining friends – the lights – fade to black. Music
dies away. It is essential that this is performed for real
– no mock heroics, no exaggerated grief. The intention
is to move the audience. House lights up. Actress alone
again, facing audience.

We hope that was moving. The intention was to
illustrate those timeless themes – death and grief. *(Long*
pause.) We think ourselves, though, that it was
nonsense. Facile. Easily assembled. You may not have
felt grief – I may not have performed convincingly
enough, but if you *did* – what aroused it? The sight of
a dead man? My rendering of a grieving wife? The
dramatic lighting? The emotion in the music? All four?
But what did you know of any of the characters? The
most important element of all was missing – language.
Nothing was said! Supposing you'd been told that the
dead man, just a few minutes earlier, had set fire to a
house full of people, a family – including children –
whom he didn't like, whom he'd just quarrelled with,
and that he'd been shot dead by the father who, with

his wife and children, was trapped in the house and had managed to shoot dead the arsonist before going up in flames with his family? Just painting that image with words out here on a bare stage with no lighting, no music, no special tone of tragedy in my voice has enabled you to experience the scene completely differently, perhaps it's even touched you more than the contrived spectacle you've just witnessed. *(Long pause. Mood of 'lecturing' thins away. Very gently:)* Now, forget what I said that scene *might* have been about.

> *Exactly the same takes place as before except there is no music: – lights – three men carrying a fourth – the wife grieving – one man turning to rage at 'those' off stage – two restraining him. One of those restraining him speaks to him:*

ONE: So? Fool! Will you go back into the crowd? Will you rage at them? Fool! No one will hear you. Stupidity is like a vampire – it has no reflection. You'll be driven to strike someone dead, they'll retaliate, another man will die and another and another and another . . . until the madness is spent. Then time will pass, and again charlatans will blossom, again the gullible idiots will listen, again they'll marvel, applaud, forget the dying and wallow in the hate. And there will be no end, dearly beloved . . . on and on and on and on and on and on and on and on and . . .

> *Music. Voice fades. Lights fade.*

SCENE TWO

FRANK McGUINNESS

An old man, Raoul, lies on the ground. A young man, Anton, sits watching him.

ANTON: Do you ever think of Sweden?

RAOUL: When I think of my father. But it is all so long ago.

Growing old is terrible, my dear. *(Birdsong)* When Papa died, four men dressed in black carried his dead body to his grave. It was the depth of winter and the grave had been dug since autumn, for we were expecting him to die. The earth was so hard in winter we had to do that in parts of Sweden. If there was a sudden death, a young person, even a child, we wrapped them in the snow.

ANTON: What happened when it melted?

RAOUL: We buried them, of course. *(Birdsong)* Birds sing. That is a sentence. One day in school a teacher told us that every sentence needed three words, a subject, a predicate and an object. A boy I loved, he said, birds sing. Why have I remembered that? I know. I dreamt of him recently. He was still young, but even in my dream, I was an old man.

ANTON: Did he still love you?

RAOUL: I said I loved him. And in the dream I still did.

ANTON: Did he love you?

RAOUL: I didn't ask him. It would not have been polite. I was a well brought up boy.

ANTON: And they don't fall in love.

RAOUL: Spare me your Russian ecstasies. They bore me.

ANTON: Mr Wallenberg is bored then?

RAOUL: Frequently.

ANTON: Shall I banish this boredom?

RAOUL: You may try.

Anton goes to Raoul and kisses him. He kneels and cradles Raoul's head in his lap. Anton's wrists are bandaged. He strokes Raoul's face.

ANTON: If Our Lord had lived, he would have resembled you.

RAOUL: From ecstasies to mysticism, my dear, I cannot keep up with you. Such violent swings of mood, you'll have me quite convinced you're an Irishman. Don't fall victim to that unfortunate fantasy. *(Raoul raises Anton's bandaged wrists to his lips and kisses them.)* You really should stop mutilating yourself. It will ruin your wrists. A pretty wrist is a young Russian's most precious asset. Keep it intact, my dear.

ANTON: They are the reason I may remain with you.

RAOUL: So you are not mad?

ANTON: No more than you.

RAOUL: I once was.

ANTON: So was I.

RAOUL: Yet you stay here.

ANTON: As have you. Why?

RAOUL: We have had this conversation before.

ANTON: Why have you stayed here?

RAOUL: I was asked to.

ANTON: You would be a hero –

RAOUL: No, I would be an example. In every generation, one just man among the Gentiles. I would justify the war. For the Allies. There were no Allies. Only enemies. I preferred the punishment of the enemy to the adulation of my allies. I didn't play the game, my dear. All games have rules, and war has more than most games. The first rule is that peace must be the consequence of war, and peace, as much as war, requires its fucking heroes. And I am no one's fucking hero in war or in peace.

ANTON: You were a saviour to many –

RAOUL: Jews? Do you know I cannot remember the face of one Jew I am said to have saved.

ANTON: The world knows otherwise, even in Russia we know –

RAOUL: I remember none of them. *(Birdsong)* I remember the face of a boy I loved at school. I remember my father's funeral. That night for dinner we ate roast turkey and apple pie. Or was that on my tenth birthday? I cannot say for sure. I'm an old man. I know nothing for sure.

ANTON: I am sorry for upsetting you, Mr Wallenberg.

RAOUL: There is no such person. He vanished after the war. It

was a consequence of war, his disappearance. I must
live with this hard fact. I am an old man in a mental
home in the middle of Russia. That is all there is to it.

    Birdsong.

ANTON: I have brought you a gift. *(From his pocket Anton
produces a knife, wrapped in bandages. He unwraps the
bandages.)* Do you like it?

RAOUL: Why should I?

ANTON: Because I'm giving it to you.

RAOUL: As a consequence of your love?

ANTON: Were you to die, and I to die with you, we would
continue living, in this knife, with which we took our
life, for after they cleaned it of blood, it would still be
useful, for cutting things. And it is imperative that our
death be useful, when our lives, as you say, have been
useless, worth only to be forgotten.

RAOUL: My dear, it is terrible to grow suicidal.

ANTON: My dear, it is terrible to grow old.

RAOUL: My father died of natural causes.

ANTON: I killed mine. *(Laughs)* I am so sorry. He was a hero. I
loved him. He fought in the war. He survived. He
escaped. You may have saved him. Thank you.

RAOUL: Yes. *(Takes the knife. As he speaks, he wraps the knife
back into the bandages.)* There was a woman, an old
woman, I met in Budapest. A Jew. I remember her
speaking to me in the most beautiful French. As a
diplomat, I was, of course, fluent in that language.
Suddenly she lowered her voice and she whispered, do
you speak English? I nodded.

ANTON: I am growing confused. Try to understand me. I must
trust you. I am so afraid of dying. There are so many
terrible stories of how we die. I do not wish to believe
them. I wish to live.

RAOUL: I wish to live, she said. Please, save me. I am an old
woman under sentence of death, and I am afraid. It is
terrible to grow old, to be afraid. It is terrible to be
under sentence of death. I could only agree with her. I

resumed our conversation in French. I started for some reason to tell her a story, by Maupassant. At the end of the story, an old man and an old woman, great artists from a lost era, dance the minuet. *(Raoul dances with the bandaged knife, jerkily, speaking as he dances.)* Like a clockwork toy, they danced. And at its end, they fell weeping into each other's arms, remembering, remembering, their youth, when they were brave, brave, dancing. Throughout the story, she said nothing. She did not look at me. Until I told her the last line *Vous trouvez cela ridicule, sans doute.* No doubt you find this ridiculous. Absolutely inconsequential, like birds singing. *(Birdsong)* I think I might have saved her, but it is doubtful.

ANTON: It may soon be time for tea.

RAOUL: How do you know?

ANTON: I can smell a samovar.

RAOUL: Good. Good. Samovars.

> *Raoul lies on the ground. Anton sits watching him. The bandaged knife lies on Raoul's stomach.*

SCENE THREE

NICHOLAS WRIGHT

Anton Pavlovich Chekhov, Konstantin Sergeivich Stanislavsky and Olga Knipper around a table. Olga Knipper is clumsily shuffling a pack of cards.

ANTON
PAVLOVICH: You flew?

KONSTANTIN
SERGEIVICH: I flew.

ANTON
PAVLOVICH: Do you mean that your train from Moscow seemed – to you – subjectively – to travel on wings? Or did you come by troika? You see, I still can't work out how you managed to arrive in Yalta before your telegram.

OLGA: If Konstantin Sergeivich says he flew, he flew.

ANTON
PAVLOVICH: Yes yes yes but – . Give me the cards, my darling. *(He takes them.)* Like all romantic actresses, my wife has a disordered relationship with the outside world.

OLGA: Like what?

ANTON
PAVLOVICH: Like you bump into furniture.

OLGA: Never on stage. Not if I do what Konstantin Sergeivich tells me. Chairs glide out of my way. Teaspoons leap into my hands.

ANTON
PAVLOVICH: Ah. *(To Konstantin Sergeivich:)* And how did you fly?

KONSTANTIN
SERGEIVICH: On a carpet.

ANTON
PAVLOVICH: *(Shuffling)* What kind of a carpet?

KONSTANTIN
SERGEIVICH: It's a – . Well how can I describe it, it's a six hundred-year-old Uzbeki prayer-mat. Deconsecrated.

ANTON
PAVLOVICH: *(Still shuffling.)* And it went all right?

KONSTANTIN
SERGEIVICH: I struck a difficult patch over Kiev.

ANTON
PAVLOVICH: Oh, I like Kiev. It's a very attractive city, were the trees in blossom?

OLGA: He couldn't *see* them. How could he *see* the trees in blossom, he was miles above them.

ANTON
PAVLOVICH: How many miles?

KONSTANTIN
SERGEIVICH: It isn't measurable in units.

ANTON
PAVLOVICH: Well, wherever you were. High up. You said you struck a difficult patch, what caused it?

KONSTANTIN
SERGEIVICH: Hostile demons.

ANTON
PAVLOVICH: Coming from where?

OLGA: Up from Kiev. He's told you a thousand times.

KONSTANTIN
SERGEIVICH: It's Ramadan.

ANTON
PAVLOVICH: Ah. Yes yes, well that would account for – . I'll deal,
shall I? Well, you're the theatre director, I suppose you
showed the demons where to stand and told them to
shut up and that's what they did.

KONSTANTIN
SERGEIVICH: They did.

ANTON
PAVLOVICH: They didn't complain?

KONSTANTIN
SERGEIVICH: *(Smiles with satisfaction.)* Oh they complained.

OLGA: Konstantin Sergeivich exercised his authority.

ANTON
PAVLOVICH: Well done. One two, one two, one two. *(He's dealing.
They're playing vingt-et-un (21 to you). Olga Knipper is
bank. Anton Pavlovich has given them all two cards each.
Now he gives the stack to his wife.)* Thank you, my
darling. One moment. *(He coughs. Takes out a
handkerchief, coughs into it. Blood on the handkerchief.
Puts the handkerchief away.)* Let's start.

OLGA: What's your stake?

ANTON
PAVLOVICH: My stake. All right, I shall or shall not tell Konstantin
Sergeivich whether or not I landed in the target area.
(To Konstantin Sergeivich:) Agreed?

KONSTANTIN
SERGEIVICH: Agreed.

He turns his cards over.

ANTON
PAVLOVICH: *(Pleasantly surprised.)* Ah. I'll buy.

OLGA: Stake please.

ANTON
PAVLOVICH: I'll tell Konstantin Sergeivich whether or not I met the object of my research. And what he was like. *(To Konstantin Sergeivich:)* Yes? *(Konstantin Sergeivich raises a hand in agreement. Olga Knipper deals Anton Pavlovich a card. He looks.)* Stick.

OLGA: *(To Konstantin Sergeivich:)* Stake please.

KONSTANTIN
SERGEIVICH: I will or will not play Hamlet. *(He turns over his cards. Looks. Pleased.)* Mm hm ha ha mm hm. I'll buy.

OLGA: Stake please.

KONSTANTIN
SERGEIVICH: What?

OLGA: What will you pay?

KONSTANTIN
SERGEIVICH: It will or will not be the greatest triumph of my career. *(Olga Knipper gives him a card.)* Bust.

Olga Knipper turns over her cards.

OLGA: Twenty.

ANTON
PAVLOVICH: Fuck.

KONSTANTIN
SERGEIVICH: Can I make that Richard the Second?

OLGA: Certainly not. *(To Anton Pavlovich:)* Pay up.

ANTON
PAVLOVICH: Very well. *(To Konstantin Sergeivich:)* You listening?

KONSTANTIN
SERGEIVICH: I'm listening.

ANTON
PAVLOVICH: I landed.

KONSTANTIN
SERGEIVICH: And?

ANTON
PAVLOVICH: It was extraordinarily cold. The food is terrible. And
the regime is brutal. Few of the inmates are insane in
any clinical sense of the word. Treatment consists of
powerful soporifics, forcibly administered. And of
wrapping the so-called patient in wet sheets, which are
then allowed to dry and to contract in the course of
doing so. This is painful. It doesn't compare with
flogging, which as you know I have also observed. At
length. An experience which afflicted me more
powerfully than any other in my life. Although I've
never employed it as a base for fiction. I doubt that
wrapping in sheets compares with flogging as a source
of animal pain. But it's most certainly punitive rather
than therapeutic. I was ashamed to be a doctor. *(To
Konstantin Sergeivich:)* Is that enough?

KONSTANTIN
SERGEIVICH: Not quite.

ANTON
PAVLOVICH: Very well. Wallenberg is alive. He is coherent. Rather a
pretentious man. He made a pass at me, did you know
he was a homosexual?

KONSTANTIN
SERGEIVICH: Of course.

ANTON
PAVLOVICH: You might have warned me. He seems to have been
incarcerated in the course of a severe historical
convulsion.

OLGA: What kind of convulsion?

ANTON
PAVLOVICH: *(Of Konstantin Sergeivich.)* Ask *him.*

OLGA: *(To Konstantin Sergeivich:)* Well?

KONSTANTIN
SERGEIVICH: I don't know. Believe me, if I did I'd tell you, but it
isn't like you suppose. The future isn't a set of tramway
lines. You can't look down the track and see the
following station. Things can change. *(They wait,
interested to see whether he has any further information on
the subject.)* All I can say, there will most probably be a

war and here in Russia a political shift of some kind,
I'm still working on it. *(To Anton Pavlovich:)* And?

ANTON
PAVLOVICH: You've had your quota. *(To Olga:)* Deal.

She deals. Two cards each.

OLGA: Stakes please.

ANTON
PAVLOVICH: I've decided to play for money.

KONSTANTIN
SERGEIVICH: That's unacceptable.

ANTON
PAVLOVICH: Why?

KONSTANTIN
SERGEIVICH: *(Smiles)* Because I don't need money.

ANTON
PAVLOVICH: Very well. I'll stake my house.

KONSTANTIN
SERGEIVICH: *(Laughs)* I don't need a house.

ANTON
PAVLOVICH: So what do you want?

KONSTANTIN
SERGEIVICH: I want you to write that play.

ANTON
PAVLOVICH: I haven't quite reached that stage. *(Thinks)* Good, fine,
             I stake that if I lose, Olga and I will have no children.

OLGA: *(Appalled)* What?

ANTON
PAVLOVICH: *(Firm)* You heard me.

OLGA: *(Still appalled.)* Jesus!

ANTON
PAVLOVICH: That's the stake. *(He turns over his cards.)* I'll stick.

OLGA: Take a card.

ANTON
PAVLOVICH: I'm sticking! *(Olga is stunned, doesn't move.)* The gentleman wants to bid.

> *She turns slowly to Konstantin Sergeivich. He speaks kindly to her.*

KONSTANTIN
SERGEIVICH: Anton Pavlovich and I have signed a pact in greasepaint. This is the price of genius. Neither of us expects you to understand it. It's gentlemen's business. Sometimes the stakes will be harsh and sometimes generous. Anton Pavlovich, I beg you not to misinterpret my motives when I say that my stake is as follows: the play you are at present writing will be a failure. *(He turns his cards over.)* Just as I hoped, a terrible hand. I'll buy.

OLGA: *(Shaking)* Your stake?

KONSTANTIN
SERGEIVICH: Not only will the play be a failure in Russian, but it will never be played in any language throughout the world. *(She gives him a card.)* Bust. I'm delighted. *(To Olga Knipper:)* Let's see you.

> *She reveals her cards.*

OLGA: Twenty-one.

ANTON
PAVLOVICH: *(Chucks his cards in.)* Fifteen.

KONSTANTIN
SERGEIVICH: *(To Olga Knipper:)* Deal. Stop snivelling.

> *She tries to. Deals everyone two new cards.*

OLGA: *(To Anton Pavlovich:)* Your stake?

ANTON
PAVLOVICH: I've nothing left.

OLGA: You know what he wants.

ANTON
PAVLOVICH: Of course, of course. He wants a play on the subject of Raoul Wallenberg.

OLGA: Then stake it.

ANTON
PAVLOVICH: No.

OLGA: Why not?

> *Pause. Anton Pavlovich coughs, stems the flow of blood. They look at him. He looks back, innocent. Konstantin Sergeivich addresses him with magisterial intensity:*

KONSTANTIN
SERGEIVICH: A man devotes his life to rescuing the victims of war. He is a Swedish aristocrat. Yet he identifies with Jews, the lowest of the oppressed. Is he rewarded? No, he disappears into a maze of mirrors, into an infinitely complex penal network. Twenty years later, he is still inside it. What are his feelings? What are his thoughts? This is a subject Sophocles would have been proud of. Who, in the present epoch, is worthier of it than yourself? I asked you to meet him. You agreed. All that remains is for you to write the play.

> *Pause. Anton Pavlovich puts his blood-stained handkerchief on the table.*

ANTON
PAVLOVICH: I stake my life.

> *They look at him, appalled.*

KONSTANTIN
SERGEIVICH: Didn't you hear what I said? Don't you think it's a wonderful idea?

ANTON
PAVLOVICH: Believe me, Konstantin Sergeivich: I can write stories. And I can write plays. But I can't write ideas. Frankly, I'd rather die.

SCENE FOUR

RICHARD CURTIS

The same characters as in the preceding section, continuing straight on.

ANTON: Believe me, Konstantin Sergeivich: I can write stories.
              And I can write plays. But I can't write ideas. Frankly
              I'd rather die.

KONSTAN-
TIN: Fair enough. I shall stop my nagging. And, in fact, if
              it's all right with you, dear Anton, I shall stop this
              game also.

ANTON: Why, have you grown tired of it?

KONSTAN-
TIN: No – but the fellow who's just taken over the play
              doesn't have a bloody clue how to play cards – and as
              you've just said, it is best to write of things we know
              about.

ANTON: True.

OLGA: Tell us then instead about the play you are going to
              work on next, dear Anton.

ANTON: No, it would bore you.

KONSTAN-
TIN: (With irony.) Be bored by one of your plays? Never.

ANTON: Very well – but you must be honest with me – tell me
              what you really think.

KONSTAN-
TIN: Of course – you know I have always been brutally
              honest with you.

ANTON: Yes indeed. Well, the first one I have planned is called
              The Four Sisters.

OLGA: Wonderful – lots of parts for the girls. What's it about?

ANTON: Well, it's about these four sisters stuck in a suffocating
              small community, desperate to leave and go to Moscow.
              One is a school teacher, one takes care of the house,
              one is young and still studying, and the fourth is a
              belly dancer at the local tavern.

KONSTAN-
TIN: Are there normally belly dancers in small Russian
              towns?

ANTON: Well, I suppose not – but I wanted to add a bit of spice.

KONSTAN-
TIN: I'd be careful. Put in one unrealistic thing, and people don't believe in anything.

ANTON: Well, perhaps you're right. Yes. Yes. Perhaps I should cut the belly dancer. Three Sisters. Yes – it could work – I rather wanted to make it four so those awful three Ptascynski sisters didn't think it was written for them – they're all totally wrong for it.

OLGA: And do they eventually go to Moscow?

ANTON: O yes – the second half is great: the belly dancer goes and joins the Moscow Circus and finally they all get jobs there – the teacher becomes the lion-tamer and the other two form a high-trapeze act. Although, of course, that'll all be difficult if I have to cut the belly dancer.

KONSTAN-
TIN: I suppose they could just stay in the town for the second half.

ANTON: No way, José – the audience would die of boredom. Still, I'll think of something.

OLGA: Tell us about the others.

ANTON: Well, there's a very good one called The Asparagus Patch.

KONSTAN-
TIN: Sounds unusual.

ANTON: Not really. It's the same sort of usual themes – a family trying to keep their old property alive under all the modern economic pressures.

OLGA: And they grow asparagus?

ANTON: Yes – well, I'm not absolutely sure. It's between that and cherries.

OLGA: So it could be The Cherry Patch?

ANTON: Yes – Cherry Orchard I suppose – or Asparagus Patch – either way, it's a cracker and there's this hilarious bit at the end with some old git being left in the house.

I'm thinking of a doing a sequel where a new couple
move in and find there's a corpse underneath the stairs.

KONSTAN-
TIN: Fun – I've always wanted to direct a thriller.

ANTON: O well, you won't like the third one I'm working on
            then. It's a real light comedy.

OLGA: What's it called?

ANTON: 'Uncle Vanya . . . and Auntie Dot'.

OLGA: What's it about?

ANTON: Well – it all starts terribly serious – this very depressed
            man, a frustrated doctor, a beautiful tortured woman . . .

KONSTAN-
TIN: That's you Olga.

            Olga acknowledges modestly.

ANTON: . . . and a sad frustrated housekeeper. And you think
            it's all going to end in maudlin disaster, when who
            should arrive but good old Auntie Dot – the cheerful
            ex-matron who perks them all up with her boisterous
            anecdotes about life at a Kiev boys' school. What do
            you think?

KONSTAN-
TIN: O, I don't know. I don't want to be tough on you,
            Anton, but these big comic turns aren't really your
            strength.

ANTON: *(A little hurt.)* Yes, so you say.

KONSTAN-
TIN: Remember what happened on 'The Seagull and The
            Hippopotamus.'

ANTON: O yes.

KONSTAN-
TIN: We had to . . .

ANTON: Cut the hippopotamus.

KONSTAN-
TIN: Who was incidentally, if I remember rightly, a jolly ex-

matron from a boy's school, who stopped the dull
youth committing suicide with her . . .

ANTON: Jolly tales from the dorm. Yes – you don't like that
character do you?

KONSTAN-
TIN: Well, no – it's just she seemed to conflict with the
general tone. All that stuff about midnight feasts and
little boys yanking on their . . .

ANTON: O all right – fuck it – I'll cut the gags and slip in
another broken heart.

KONSTAN-
TIN: Play to your strengths, Anton.

ANTON: Well, anyway, I can't do anything for the moment.

OLGA: Another short story.

ANTON: No – I got this long letter from Leo Tolstoy about a
week ago, and I've got to write back.

KONSTAN-
TIN: And how's old Leo?

ANTON: O complaining a lot – apparently he's having no end of
trouble with "Peace".

OLGA: The novel?

ANTON: Yes – he's thinking of adding a few chapters about the
actual fighting. Thinks he might have to change the
title.

OLGA: You poor writers. Well, I'll be off. There is one last
thing though.

ANTON: What's that darling Olga?

OLGA: Well, to pay you back for stealing all the good lines in
this scene, I've put poison in the tea. You've both got
two minutes to live. Bye.

SCENE FIVE

TARIQ ALI

All except three male actors are back on stage sitting in a large circle.
They are all watching an inner circle of five men and two women.
Everyone is looking extremely depressed. The talking now is done by the
Inner Circle.

FIRST MAN: Just as I thought. A pile of crap. Then they attack us
for not putting this trash on the stage. I mean I'm not
at all sympathetic to this government. I've fought the
Arts Council for years, but not for this . . .

SECOND
MAN: These are bad times. The Minister promised he would
rescue us and he did. What a fate, eh! A large rep in
the middle of a tourist Disneyland in the Midlands.
They've given us more money than we've ever
received . . .

THIRD MAN: Hands on or Hands off?

SECOND
MAN: Hands gone! But we must repay their trust in us.
Quality and caution. That's my motto.

FIRST
WOMAN: It's terrible. I know. What can we do?

FOURTH
MAN: Look, we all know the problem. We are prisoners of
this fucking enterprise culture.

SECOND
WOMAN: I feel like an internal exile. But . . . what can we do
except wait for better times.

FIFTH MAN: The Professor's late.

FIRST
WOMAN: The trains are always late from Oxford these days.

FOURTH
MAN: Are you sure he's coming?

FIRST
WOMAN: Oh yes. I spoke to him this morning. He's new and
              eager.

FIRST MAN: The last time we were addressed by the Oxford
              Professor of English, Ken Tynan walked out and the
              actors rioted.

              Enter a bespectacled Professor. It is Terry Eagleton,
              Wharton Professor of English at Oxford. He is
              beaming and has a sheaf of paper in his hand.

EAGLETON: Sorry for being late. The train made an unscheduled
              stop at Ealing Broadway. Crowds were dancing on the
              tracks. *(Chuckles)* On the tracks of Historical
              Materialism, eh? *(Winks)* No more fugitive cant. Let's
              stop being refugees in our own country. Well, friends, I
              had prepared an erudite talk. Deconstructing
              Shakespeare. Reconstructing Oscar Wilde, but forget all
              that. Here is a little ditty I wrote a long time ago.
              (Hands the sheets to everyone.) Rather apposite now, I
              think. Should we have a go. By the way it's to the tune
              of Land of Hope and Glory and I have tentatively
              called it the Ballad of English Literature.

              All stand up and sing except Inner Circle which
              remains shell-shocked.

ALL: Chaucer was a class traitor;
              Shakespeare hated the mob.
              Donne sold out a bit later;
              Sidney was a nob.

              Marlowe was an elitist;
              Ben Jonson was much the same.
              Bunyan was a defeatist;
              Dryden played the game.

              There's a sniff of reaction
              About Alexander Pope;
              Sam Johnson was a Tory
              And Walter Scott a dope.

              Coleridge was a right winger;
              Keats was lower middle class.
              Wordsworth was a cringer,
              But William Blake was a gas.

Dickens was a reformist;
Tennyson was a blue.
Disraeli was mostly pissed
And nothing that Trollope said was true.

Willy Yeats was a fascist,
So were Eliot and Pound;
Lawrence was a sexist,
Virginia Woolf was unsound.

There are only three names
To be plucked from this dismal set:
Milton, Blake and Shelley
Will smash the ruling class yet.

Milton, Blake and Shelley
Will smash the ruling class yet.

THE END